BY RAY BRADBURY

WHERE ROBOT MICE
AND ROBOT MEN
RUN ROUND IN ROBOT TOWNS

RAY BRADBURY

WHERE

NEW POEMS,

ROBOT MICE

BOTH

AND

LIGHT

ROBOT MEN

AND

RUN ROUND

DARK

IN ROBOT TOWNS

ALFRED · A · KNOPF · NEW YORK · 1977

THIS IS A BORZOI BOOK

PUBLISHED BY ALFRED A. KNOPF, INC.

Published in the United States
by Alfred A. Knopf, Inc., New York,
and simultaneously in Canada
by Random House of Canada Limited, Toronto.
Distributed by Random House, Inc., New York.
Library of Congress Cataloging in Publication Data
Bradbury, Ray [date]
Where robot mice and robot men run round
in robot towns.
I. Title.
PS3503.R167W54   811'.5'4   77-77539
ISBN 0-394-42206-6
Manufactured in the United States of America
First Edition

Again for Marguerite/Maggie—because of thirty-two years

They asked me where I'd choose to run, which favored? Ups?
    or Downs?
Where robot mice and men, I said, run round in robot towns.
But is that wise? for tin's a fool and iron has no thought!
Computer mice can find me facts and teach me what I'm not.
But robot all inhuman is, all's sin with cog and mesh.
Not if we teach the good stuff in, so *it* can teach our flesh.
There's nothing wrong with metal-men that better dreams
    can't chalk.
I'd find me robot-Plato's cave if he lived on my block;
And though his eyes electric were, computerized his tongue,
Is that more wrong than Berlioz on LPs harped and sung?
So much electric fills our lives, some bad, some good, some
    ill.
But look! there Shaw and Shakespeare dance on Channel 7's
    sill:
A gift of hearts and minds and eyes to see our dark/light face,
To weigh and balance halos/blights that half-destroy our race;
To midget make our rocket-ships, and squeeze grand Kong
    down small
Then Giants grow from Shavian seed to taunt, provoke us all.
As man himself a mixture is, rambunctious paradox,
So we must teach our mad machines: stand tall, pull up your
    socks!
Come run with me, wild children/men, half dires and dooms,
    half clowns.
Pace robot mice, race robot men, win-lose in robot towns.

WHERE ROBOT MICE
AND ROBOT MEN
RUN ROUND IN ROBOT TOWNS

Byzantium
I come not from
But from another time and place
Whose race is simple, tried and true;
As boy
I dropped me forth in Illinois,
A name with neither love nor grace
Was Waukegan. There I came from
And not, good friends, Byzantium.
And yet in looking back I see
From topmost part of farthest tree
A land as bright, beloved and blue
As any Yeats found to be true.
The house I lived in, hewn of gold
And on the highest market sold
Was dandelion-minted, made
By spendthrift bees in bee-loud glade.
And then of course our finest wine
Came forth from that same dandelion,
While dandelion was my hair
As bright as all the summer air;
I dipped in rainbarrels for my eyes
And cherries stained my lips, my cries,
My shouts of purest exaltation:
Byzantium? No. That Indian nation
Which made of Indian girls and boys
Spelled forth itself as Illinois.
Yet all the Indian bees did hum:

Byzantium.
Byzantium.

So we grew up with mythic dead
To spoon upon midwestern bread
And spread old gods' bright marmalade
To slake in peanut-butter shade.
Pretending there beneath our sky
That it was Aphrodite's thigh;
Pretending, too, that Zeus was ours
And Thor fell down in thundershowers.
While by the porch-rail calm and bold
His words pure wisdom, stare pure gold
My grandfather a myth indeed
Did all of Plato supersede;
While Grandmama in rocking-chair
Sewed up the raveled sleeve of care,
Crocheted cool snowflakes rare and bright
To winter us on summer night.
And uncles gathered with their smokes
Emitted wisdoms masked as jokes,
And aunts as wise as Delphic maids
Dispensed prophetic lemonades
To boys knelt there as acolytes
On Grecian porch on summer nights.
Then went to bed there to repent
The evils of the innocent

The gnat-sins sizzling in their ears
Said, through the nights and through the years
Not Illinois nor Waukegan
But blither sky and blither sun;
Though mediocre all our Fates
And Mayor not as bright as Yeats
Yet still we knew ourselves. The sum?
Byzantium.
Byzantium.

What I do is me—for that I came.
What I do is *me!*
For *that* I came into the world!
So said Gerard;
So said that gentle Manley Hopkins.
In his poetry and prose he saw the Fates that chose
Him in genetics, then set him free to find his way
Among the sly electric printings in his blood.
God thumbprints thee! he said.
Within your hour of birth
He touches hand to brow, He whorls and softly stamps
The ridges and the symbols of His soul above your eyes!
But in that selfsame hour, full born and shouting
Shocked pronouncements of one's birth,
In mirrored gaze of midwife, mother, doctor
See that Thumbprint fade and fall away in flesh
So, lost, erased, you seek a lifetime's days for it
And dig deep to find the sweet instructions there
Put by when God first circuited and printed thee to life:
"Go hence! do this! do that! do yet another thing!
This self is yours! Be *it!*"
And what is that?! you cry at hearthing breast,
Is there no rest? No, only journeying to be yourself.
And even as the Birthmark vanishes, in seashell ear
Now fading to a sigh, His last words send you in the world:
"Not mother, father, grandfather are you.
Be not another. Be the self I signed you in your blood.

I swarm your flesh with you. Seek that.
And, finding, be what no one else can be.
I leave you gifts of Fate most secret; find no other's Fate,
For if you do, no grave is deep enough for your despair
No country far enough to hide your loss.
I circumnavigate each cell in you
Your merest molecule is right and true.
Look there for destinies indelible and fine
And rare.
Ten thousand futures share your blood each instant;
Each drop of blood a cloned electric twin of you.
In merest wound on hand read replicas of what I planned
    and knew
Before your birth, then hid it in your heart.
No part of you that does not snug and hold and hide
The self that you will be if faith abide.
What you do is thee. For that I gave you birth.
Be that. So be the only you that's truly you on Earth."

Dear Hopkins. Gentle Manley. Rare Gerard. Fine name.
What we do is *us*. Because of you. For *that* we came.

I AM THE RESIDUE

OF ALL MY DAUGHTERS' LIVES

Though Queen be gone, the drones come back to hives;
I am the residue of all my daughters' lives.
I keep their old loves here, I am the friend
Of all the lost, the sad, discarded, gone, made end.
Their husbands are now mine, their lovers keep
In touch with me, they telephone to weep
On loves that, soon as lost, now are my kin.
Somehow the old sins, shunted off, wind up my sin.
I take those loves to lunch. I buy them wine;
Although these boys-grown-men were never mine.
What is this thing in me which, dumb, demands
The keeping up of face, outstretch of hands?
Why must I tend their graveyard with chill stones,
Why say hello to those young bags of bones?
Those scuttled marriages gone sour or dead
Whose ruin runs my blood and cramps my head—
Why should I dine this mortuary gang,
Why not pay out Time's rope and let them hang?
Because, because, well now, again because—
Mayhap I drown in male's dread menopause,
And tend to see my face in these I dine
To drink too much of sad lust's mortal wine.
Oh, women often cry they were sore used
But these boy/men were much the same abused;
If men shunt off the fainter sex with guile
Why, women, daggerless, slay with a smile.
What do these lovers hope to gain from me?

An echo of her flesh now found at tea,
The sounding of her voice but dimly heard
Her beauty ricocheted and drowned, absurd
In maze of old genetics yet there kept,
Some wakening of love that now is slept?
An echo of her voice in some mere phrase,
A flicker of her glance in old beast's gaze?
They come to find the lamb in lion's paws,
But something in my laugh now gives them cause
To order more and more and deeply drink,
Though Lovely's not my name, I clearly think.
Ah, well, to stand for her is not a shame,
And if the echo pleases them, what blame?
Years back I saw an old love's sire one day,
And round about his smile I saw the fey
Sad, far, lost echoing of one mad year
Which ravened me to frenzies and wild fear.
So if a father's teeth can cage a cat,
Why here behind my eyes, beneath my hat,
A girl before her time waits to commence—
Young men, I have no heart to cry: Go hence!
So stay awhile and hear her voice in me;
But, please, no tears, no funeral salt at tea!

Thrown out of Eden
Now we headlong humans
Sinners sinned against
Return.
Tossed from the central sun
We with our own concentric fires
Blaze and burn.
Once at the hub of wakening
And vast starwheel,
For centuries long-lost, and made to feel
Unwanted, orphaned, mindless,
Driven forth to grassless gardens,
Dead and desert sea,
We were shut out by comet grooms like Kepler
Galileo Galilei
Whose short-sight probing light-years
Upped and said:
The Hub's not here!
So shot man through the head
And worse, each starblind prophet killed a part,
Snugged shut our souls,
Chopped short our reach,
Entombed our living heart.
But now we bastard sons of time
Pronounce ourselves anew
And strike fire-hammer blows
To change tomorrow's clime, its meteor snows.
Our rocket selfhood grows

To give dull facts a shake, break data down
To climb the Empire State and thundercry the town;
But more! reach up and strike
And claim from Heaven
The Garden we were shunted from,
For now, space-driven
We fit, fix, force and fuse,
Re-hub the systems vast
Respoke starwheel
And at the spiraled core
Plant foot, full fire-shod
And thus saints feel
Or yeast like flesh of God.
We march back to Olympus,
Our plain-bread flesh burns gold!
We clothe ourselves in flame
And trade new myths for old.
The Greek gods christen us
With ghosts of comet swords;
God smiles and names us thus:
"Arise! Run! Fly, my *Lords!*"

It was a smother of Time, a crumbling of white;
The night gave way in hysterias trembling to cold,
Grown old and falling apart, let its white heart go
And slow and slow in a withering slide from the dark
The snow fell down and down with no lantern nor spark
Nor star nor moon to show its fracture and fall
Appalling in all its shivering shaken chill dusts
In soft clamors and tremors of panic it touched my sill
Like an old woman begging the storm to keep warm with
     mere crusts
And make do on my cat-couching hearth
Where a teakettle cinnamon puss kneels and folds
And beholds a soft inner contentment, a bumblebee simmer
     kept there
Like a hive on the hearth in a honeycomb color of cat
While nibbling the windows and gnawing raw rainspout toes
And flaking the rainbarrel frost there the smothering goes;
A funeral quell passes by in a pageant of lost
And cataracts windowpane eyes with a filming of frost
And sugars the dogs as they yellow-write sums in the snow—
Strange Orient alphabets sprinkled where smiling dogs go.
And the winter's old bones fall apart in a shatter of white
And I bed with my bumblebee honeycomb cat for the night
And the sound of the snow grows in heart-murmur patterns
     yet dimmer
And the one thing I hear in deep sleep is the motor of cat:
What sound's that?
Long-lost summer.

Oh, pantry Deeps' miscellany
Bestirs boy's victual villainy,
Unwaters mouth of innocence,
Unshucks the soul of reticence;
For in the deeps of snowbin sweets
And hung-banana jungle treats
We wandered as a jump-squirrel boy
To amble, maunder, ponder, toy
With jellies, jams and other pelf
From apple-cherry-berry shelf,
And read the names and wondered how
Clown doughnuts lay in such deep snow;
And took cosmetic chocolate-chips
To draw moustache on virgin lips.
And full of candied avarice
Blacked-out our teeth with licorice,
And grinned like devilled ham at self
Preserved in mirror-jars on shelf
And saw our eyes gone berry-blue
As all the jams this summer grew,
And bright our lips as cherry sins
And ripe our smile as pumpkin grins;
And full our mind of murder/slaughter
But clean our breath as menthol water

That in the dripped night, dark and still
The old dog laps from icebox sill.

Boy Pope behold! Dog Bishop see!
Twin celebrants in dark pantry
Where all the pontiff's orbs are kept:
Crabapple multitudes, sweet slept.
Confessional the cubby seems
Where dog and boy feed naked dreams
And wash it all in innocence
From parsley/pickle/peppermints,
To in the half-lit wild of dawn
Uncoil in cartwheels on the lawn
And teach drab cats to catnip take
And Christian fasts call forth and break.
Then up the stairs the saved child creeps
And icebox-hid the sly dog sleeps
And none to know their midnight sins
Are stashed and slept in pantry bins.

And what the moral in this lies?
Stop boys. Leash dogs. Swat bugs. Squash flies.
Prohibit such from pantry reach,
Or they will salt the sugar teach,

And rum the apple, gin the pear
With summer sins grown unaware:
God finds at Year's End what was His
Now Lucifer's wine-cellar is.

But . . . Sh! Abed the sweet boy dogs,
And dog like boy-in-brambly-togs
Beneath the icebox laps the gin
Of melted Snow Maiden within;
And boy all purrs and golden-curled
Dreams what?

Of blowing up the world.

I have a brother, mostly dead
And angels curled upon his head;
Most of my life, mostly unseen,
And yet I feel with him I've been
A cohort playmate friend of Poe
Who tours me where live friends can't go.
He teaches me his mortal park
And where the firefly stops for spark
And how the shade within the night
Is a most fine delicious fright.
I give him words, he gives me bone
To play like Piper when alone;
And so my brother, dead, you see
Is wondrous literate company.
Thus if my Muse says: Nevermore!
I hear a tapping at my door;
My brother comes to saviour me
With graveyard biscuit, rictus tea,
That tea in which, perused awhile
One finds a lovely mummy's smile
And then again, he bids me snuff
Egyptian dusts—one pinch enough
To knock my timbers, sneeze my brain
So Idea Ghosts sit up again
To tap my eyelids, tick my nose
And shape themselves with words for clothes.
All this my long lost brother does,

This sibling spent before my cause.
He moves my hand and Lo! O Lord!
His tombstone my Ouija Board.
He shouts: Stay not in buried room,
Come forth, sweet brother, flower my tomb
With words so rare and phrase so bright
They'll bonfire burn away the night.
All this to me lost brother is
And I his live sweet Lazarus.
His shout ignore? his cry refuse?
No, no! Much thanks, long-dead fine Muse.

Why Mars?

Why go to find the place?

The human race gives answer, finds a pause,

And, no, not just Because It's There.

We walk the air from here to planet out beyond

Because we're more than fond of life and what we are.

And what is that? you ask.

For answer, go to Shaw,

Dear G.B.S. speaks constantly,

Asks Why and What are we?

The Life Force in the Universe

That longs to See!

That would Become

And in the act of being, changing, seeing, touching, growing

Looms up as beast that knows itself

And knows it knows and keeps on knowing.

We are the Abyss Light that comes from Pleiades

The stuff that, born in dark,

Now sees and knows it sees.

A mute flesh lately found and given tongue

To sing strange songs that till our time remained unsung.

And what the song, the tune?

To fashion fires and thus outrace the Moon

And with our new flame-tossing Ra-Egyptian chariot cars

Fly off to land, taste, touch and know strange Mars.

And with the knowledge gained make lasting yeast

To grow man ten ways tall to feast

On universe and stars
And use as seedbed–station–birthing place
This empty Mars.
Again: What is this perturbed flesh, dissatisfied
That longs to try and test what none have tried?
Why: Force and Matter, changed to Thought and Will
That Thought which dreams of flight in fire
To stand us Kings on Martian hill.
We Saviour call ourselves from earthly tomb
And go to find a better place, a larger room.
Mars but a Beginning,
Real Heaven our end,
That is the power man has to build and send
To answer Job's most rank despair and old outcry:
Man need not fade and fall and, falling, die!
Why Mars? Why Viking Lander on its way?
To landfall Time, give man Forever's Day . . .
Unlock the doors of light-year grave
Fling wide the portal;
Give man the gift of stars,
Grow him immortal.
Put down the Dark, kill final Death,
And sweeten Man with everlasting breath.

Know only Real? Fall dead.

So Nietzsche said.

We have our Arts so we won't die of Truth.

The World is too much with us.

The Flood stays on beyond the Forty Days.

The sheep that graze in yonder fields are wolves.

The clock that ticks inside your head is truly Time

And in the night will bury you.

The children warm in bed at dawn will leave

And take your heart and go to worlds you do not know.

All this being so

We need our Arts to teach us how to breathe

And beat our blood; accept the Devil's neighborhood,

And age and dark and cars that run us down,

And clown with Death's-head in him

Or skull that wears Fool's crown

And jingles blood-rust bells and rattles groans

To earthquake-settle attic bones late nights.

All this, this, this, all this—too much!

It cracks the heart!

And so? Find Art.

Seize brush. Take stance. Do fancy footwork. Dance.

Run race. Try poem. Write play.

Milton does more than drunk God can

To justify Man's way toward Man.

And maundered Melville takes as task

To find the mask beneath the mask.

And homily by Emily D. shows dust-bin Man's anomaly.
And Shakespeare poisons up Death's dart
And of gravedigging hones an art.
And Poe divining tides of blood
Builds Ark of bone to sail the flood.
Death, then, is painful wisdom tooth;
With Art as forceps, pull that Truth,
And plumb the abyss where it was
Hid deep in dark and Time and Cause.
Though Monarch Worm devours our heart,
With Yorick's mouth cry "Thanks!" to Art.

Poor world that does not know its doom, the day I die.
Two hundred million pass within my hour of passing,
I take this continent with me into the grave.
They are most brave, all-innocent, and do not know
That if I sink then they are next to go.
So in the hour of death they Good Times cheer
While I, mad egotist, ring in their Bad New Year.
The lands beyond my land are vast and bright,
Yet I with one sure hand put out their light.
I snuff Alaska, doubt Sun King's France, slit Britain's throat,
Promote old Mother Russia out of mind with one fell blink,
Shove China off a marble quarry brink,
Knock far Australia down and place its stone,
Kick Japan in my stride. Greece? quickly flown.
I'll make it fly and fall, as will green Eire,
Turned in my sweating dream, I'll Spain despair,
Shoot Goya's children dead, rack Sweden's sons,
Crack flowers and farms and towns with sunset guns.
When my heart stops, the great Ra drowns in sleep,
I bury all the stars in Cosmic Deep.
So, listen, world, be warned, know honest dread.
When I grow sick, that day your blood is dead.
Behave yourself, I'll stick and let you live.
But misbehave, I'll take what now I give.
That is the end and all. Your flags are furled . . .
If I am shot and dropped? So ends your world.

My love, she weeps at many things,
I would not for the world stop up her tears;
She came in many years of drought
And taught me just how right was private rain
To touch the dust with smallest storm
With emeralds dropping from her eyes.
My loved one weeps at many things,
Small rings and charms, the soft alarms of birds
Or sudden summer squall. Large thing or small:
The way the cat puts up his bones in fur,
Teakettle purrs and murmurs:
Slumber. Sleep. October. Autumn. Fall.
Sometimes I say a thing and do not know I say a Joy
Then hear a sound and turn and there she goes full-weep.
Pours forth the diamonds, lets out a cry
As from a thousand hours of happy/nightmare sleep.

In all the splendid time ahead, those years
With yet their secret joys unsaid,
Let no one stay her tears.
Praise God for them and her, praise God for eyes
That smallness see and grow it to a size,
That see in me a fellow weeper found
And celebrate by laying dust
On our small ceremonial trysting ground.
Then am I rich?
Look here . . . I wear with grace

The gifts of rain and light and love and time
She's made and winked and left
To brighten my soul's face.

Oh, would we talk of it?
It is the very staff of life to kids:
Grand Death which cheats now this, now that,
Now maid, now man at randy games,
And claims what one has won with no regrets,
Apologies, forewarnings
That times will come when evenings and mornings
Grow most still to muffle up your ears with earth,
Fill mouth with dust, quicksand your eyes
And cotton-tamp your nostrils,
Bind your feet and hands with mummy-grass of silence,
Smother tongue to mother dark's dumb songs, which sung
Collapse the bellows of your lung,
Then, stashed like moron note in envelope of Earth,
Fresh mailed, fresh bought
By night, you're bound for Nil, arrive at Naught.
The thrill of sweetening their talk with Death
And wild extinctions can make up an evening of chat
Or half a year to boys and girls
Who jump at this ripe news and nose the kill;
All innocent sniff blood, admire Dracula
And think the Monster neat.
Death is a candy treat to such and all and more.
And Life? My God! Like Mom and Dad at lunch . . .
Nice folks. But . . . *what* a bore!

The paths are empty now and gone and sunk to grass
Where we once passed and laid the track and showed the
    ways
Through summer days, my Indian brother with his cowardly
    cur,
This laggard blood who woke him summer dawns
With yawns that smelled of Clark bars or fermented Nehi pop.
They say that Time must have a stop. Well, stop it has:
I came to see the old ravine last week, some forty years
    beyond
My traveling there with Skip and Tom and Al:
The well is green, but no one shouts to hear it stir;
The trees are tall but no one apemans up the boughs;
The clouds run paths in weed, but no boys run.
Is this the setting of the sun of Earth?
I turn to look at houses, streets and town and want to cry:
Why no one here in Deeps, for Christ's sake, why?
No falling down the hill, no digging caves,
No redskin braves assaulting crayfish, hurling arrows,
Building dam?
But then I am
An old man now, and so perhaps I misremember
Climbing ivies, making swings. Oh, God's sweet blood,
A million-dozen multitudes of summer things!
Here where we pissed our names in sand and crossed the t's.
Here under bridge the Opera Phantom waited
On star-dark nights like these

When Skip and I ran home afraid down dank ravine
Each street a shadowed tombyard from a movie scene.
What, nothing here? No yells, no boys, no treehuts in the sky?
Affronted, stunned, appalled,
I blink my eyes, again ask: Why?

My driver, close behind me on the hill,
Appraises Deeps and Green and me, old man grown still.
Perhaps, he says, the boys today have better things to do.

I want to whirl. I stop my fist.
My heart is torn by TV catalyst.
I stand a moment longer, staring down
The summer winds. Spider antennae swarm the town.
From far doors I hear soughing giveaways.
I know at noons
The boys that I am seeking find cartoons
And hide in houses like sea-creatures under rock,
And with their parents, feet encased in Cronkite,
Watch NO NEWS at six o'clock.

Hearing this and seeing houses shut and strange,
I give an ancient cry, run down the hill, and make the range
From this side to the other of the Deep
And with shoes drowned in creek-spring waters, stand and
    weep.

Far off I think I hear my mother's old tin-whistle shriek,

Skirl, long-lost but endless calling: Come!
So the last old boy of time and summer-sleeps
Now feeling foolish, shoes in hand,
Makes final path and treads the milkweed
Upward from sweet wilds and Deeps.
And so on Home.

Who were those people on the summer porch in '28
And '29, smoking cigars, munching Eskimo pies,
Sneaking into the night kitchen to have a little beneath-the-
    icebox
Dog-drink of wild-grape wine?
A gathering of saints and caliphs from the East
Fresh from a feast of Grandma's biscuits
Dripped in honey fresh as summer morn?
Did any of them guess, seeing me somersault on the dark
    lawn
That I was the Christ reborn?
If so, they never said, and took the secret to the grave.
Meanwhile I was brave, waiting to grow up
And prove a miracle or two,
Kill all the mosquitoes of August,
Cause vanilla ice cream to replenish itself
Mysteriously in iceboxes in the middle of sleepless July
Nights.
Clear the attic of ghosts.
Oh, what boasts would be mine!
We all grew up or grew old or fell dead or went away.
Nobody does quite as he pleases, said Grandma.
And me? Did I become Jesus?
Almost. Not quite.
Though even now there are times at three in the morn
I almost feel I'm Him reborn.
In a winter-cold bed I'm as warm as toast

And feel like a dipper of Holy Ghost.
I call to the Bureau. Take off, fly! Well, then, creep.
The Bureau won't budge. It does as it pleases.
I cry out, "Oh, fudge," and, one more failed Jesus,
Fall down into sleep.

O child, they said, avert your eyes.

Avert my eyes? I said, what, from wild skies

Where stars appear and wheel

And fill my heart and make me feel as if I might

This night and then another and another

Live forever and not die?

Turn off my gaze, shut off my will and soul from this?

This fiery bliss and joy which tempts me to steal forth

At two a.m. and lie upon the lawn,

A boy alone with Universe

With song and verse of God spelled overhead

For me to read and know and sing;

Not know all this, go blind?

Why, God minds me to be so. He put the bright sparks in
  my blood

Which spirit, lighten, flare and frighten me to love.

Small sparks, large Sun—

All one, it is the same.

Large flame or small

I know and keep it all in eye, in heart, in mind.

The flavor of the night lies on my tongue. I speak it so

That others, uninviting of themselves, abed, not brave, may
  know

What this boy knows and will forever know:

The Universe is thronged with fire and light,

And we but smaller suns which, skinned, trapped and kept

Enshrined in blood and precious bones,

Hold back the night.

I   The Beast

The great ape falls, and Beauty sees him go.
He's dead before he hits the street and does not know
We greet his fall with tears.
The years are long since first we saw him dead.
With dread we called him Kong,
With love, sweet Beast his other name.
And Beauty, from the myth, his kith and kin.
His sin was loving without thought,
But he bought time by scaling up our dreams
To rave in clouds and send the airships down in fire.
We do desire to be like him and her
The lover and the loved above the town, apart
And then, if need be, down we go, all secret shot through
    heart.

The sound of his concussion ran before,
Oh, how he tore the sky and wounded souls
And changed fair children's minds in candy dark.
And still we fall with him, love maddened ape
[And boys who share the fall]
From her who saw him go.
We run our deaths and loves again, again
With flickered flint and spark of film
That starts us up anew where lizards wait
And Kong still vast upon his isle
And Beauty's gift to him some untouched Fate.

The bastions fall, and Brute stands at the gate
And thunders chest with fists and shouts his love,
There stop the film! Put off the final reel!
I'd see him there forever frozen, free to feel himself
The emperor of island, world, and me.
Fillet the airplanes' bones; discharge their men.
I will not see great Beast fall down again.
Thank Christ for films whose Resurrections, humming
Call forth with light: Reel One. And Kong.
And, look! . . . The Second Coming.

II The Tiger

Or at the bottom of the stair we light the scene
And then look up at Norma Desmond dressed in madness
Like a gown, a thing of diamonds and dreams,
A seamless fit without a stitch that turns and spins
Like ballroom lights, mad sins that catch the stars and fire
     them back.
"Ready," we whisper, "for," we call, "your," we murmur,
"Closeup, Norma." So we finish out the phrase.
And Norma, lost in other days, yet hears the summons
To be mad-but-with-a-purpose for a while.
Her smile is broken, then is fixed.
Her gaze is fractured
But then swiftly mends itself and finds
That he who calls from down below is lover lost
Still blind with love, late on in time, and calling hence:

"Commence. Start up. Act, be alive again."
And Norma-within-Norma-mazed-in-Norma rises firm
And surfacing, remembers lines, and moves,
Descends, and all the mute reporters like a court
And she the lovely-lost and last of queens.
All eyes are filled with tears. She takes and preens
Them round her neck as rightful gift
And coming down the stair the music towers;
She mists and flowers the frame. She fills the room.
She fills the soul and heart.
All light and time now sleep.
It says: THE END
And credits we can't read.
Gone mad in final dark, we weep.

Why didn't someone tell me about crying in the shower?
What a fair fine place to cry,
What a rare place to let go
And know that no one hears—
Let fall your tears which, with the rain that falls,
Appall nobody save yourself, and standing there
You wear your sadness, properly assuaged,
Your head and face massaged by storms of spring
Or, if you think it, autumn rain.
You drain yourself away to naught, then move to joy;
But sadness must come first, it must be bought.
A thirst for melancholy, then, must find a place
To stand in corners and know grief;
The last leaf on the tree may turn you there,
Or just the way the wind, with cats,
Prowls down the garden grass,
Or some boy passing on a bike,
Selling the end of summer with a shout,
Or some toy left like doubt upon a walk,
Or some girl's smile that, heedless, cracks the heart,
Or that cold moment when each part and place and room
In all your house is empty, still,
Your children gone, their warm rooms chill,
Their summer-oven beds unyeasted, flat,

Waiting for cats to visit some half-remembered ghost
In the long fall.
So, for absolutely no good reason at all
Old oceans rise
One's eyes are filled with salt;
Something unknown then dies and must be mourned.
Then standing beneath the shower at noon or night
Is right and proper and good—
What was not understood now comes to hand . . .
One's interior land is wonderfully nourished by tears:
The years that you brought to harvest
Are properly scythed down and laid,
The games of love you played are ribboned and filed,
A whole life locked in your blood is thus let free, unbound.
So freely found then, know it, let it go
From out your eyes and with the sweet rains flow.

But now, good boys, strong gentlemen, take heed;
This stuff is not for women, lost, alone;
The need is yours as well as theirs.
Take women's wisdom for your own.
Take sorrow's loan and let your own cares free.
Christ, give it a try!
Not to learn how to weep is, lost fool,

But to learn how to die.
Stand weeping there from midnight until morn,
Then from impacted wisdom shorn, set free,
Leap forth to laugh in freshborn Children's Hour and shout:
Oh, damn you, maids, *that's* what it's all about?!
Sweet widows with your wisdom, blast you all to hell!
Why?
Why, why, God, oh why,
Why wouldn't someone *tell* me about crying in the shower?

Somewhere a band is playing,
Playing the strangest tunes,
Of sunflower seeds and sailors
Who tide with the strangest moons.
Somewhere a drummer simmers
And trembles with times forlorn
Remembering days of summer
In Futures yet unborn.
Futures so far they are ancient
And filled with Egyptian dust,
That smell of the tomb and the lilac,
And seed that is spent from lust,
And peach that is hung on a tree-branch
Far out in the sky from one's reach,
There mummies as lovely as lobsters
Remember old Futures and teach.
And children sit by on the stone floor
And draw out their lives in the sands,
Remembering deaths that won't happen
In Futures unseen in far lands.
Somewhere a band is playing
Where the moon never sets in the sky
And nobody sleeps in the summer
And nobody puts down to die;
And Time then just goes on forever
And hearts then continue to beat
To the sound of the old moon-drum drumming

And the glide of Eternity's feet;
Where beauty is beauty eternal
And life is warm blood under skin
And fresh is the rose with life vernal
Which never knows darkness and sin.
Somewhere the memory lingers,
Somewhere the gods know death,
But birth themselves new with sweet hungers
To slake in the brook-morning's breath.
Somewhere the old people wander
And linger themselves into noon
And sleep in the wheatfields yonder
To rise as fresh children with moon.
Somewhere the children, old, maunder
And know what it is to be dead
And turn in their weeping to ponder
Oblivions filed 'neath their bed.
Somewhere the in-between people
Walk center-lines down summer street
And gaze in the crazed-mirror faces
Of opposite people they meet.
Two races pass roundabout now
With the in-between people trapped there,
To houses of faith or of doubt now
Turned weathers both stormy and fair,
And sit at the long dining table
Where Life makes a banquet of flesh,

Where dis-able makes itself able
And spoiled puts on new masks of fresh.
Somewhere a band is playing
Oh listen, oh listen, that tune!
If you learn it you'll dance on forever
In June . . .
       and yet June . . .
          and more . . . June . . .
And Death will be dumb and not clever
And Death will lie silent forever
In June and yet June and more June.

Poem written on learning that trans-Egyptian railroad firemen sometimes used mummies for locomotive cordwood

Did they do *that?*
Stoke furnaces with shrouds,
With clouds of mummy-dust and old kings, too?
Across Egyptian sands on railroad paths
Long, long ago when trains were new?
Amidst the oldness of raw dunes, worn pyramids
DDid trans-Egyptian stokers, running low on fuel,
Turn roundabout and summon Tut or Hotep's sons
And feed them in the fire, make pyre and burn a royalty?
They did.
Or so I've heard.
Absurd.
They stopped along the way and snitched a tomb, six tombs.
At ten times twenty stations (named for Styx) called
All Aboards! to plenty of ripe lords and ladies there
Strewn forth by death four thousand years before.
All folk were mummified, of course, and not just kings and
        queens;
The common sheep whose sleeps were common as the
        dust that gleans
Were there in harvest windrows scythed by lusty death;
Like kindling all about they hid in millioned graves.
So when the train puffed up and ocean-tidal-smoked
While waiting to be fed—the dead, sand-drowned,

Were handy stokings and wry faggots for the fire.
Their rictus smiles did naught for them;
The mummies, grinning with their grins
Were flung in locomotive bins;
Ten mummies at a time popped in
To make St. Elmo's iron firewheels spin.
Like holy loaves they baked in steams
Or flew in winged papyrus dreams tossed up
Like midnight ravens, charcoal rooks,
Old Alexandria's finest books set fire by fools,
Those graduates of Caesar's dumb Praetorian schools.
A pageantry of raped sheaves breathed self-consume.
From locomotive Hades, swift Hell's flume.

From Cairo south the mummy-fields were bled
And to the gorge of rushing Baal the linens fed
And scarabs wrapped in tar were from the porch
Of ancient tombs seized forth to bandage torch,
Light hierarchies of Time and, one by one,
With mighty Ra, fall in that final Sun,
That Sun which in the bosom of steam-beast
Of Tyre and Ptolemy makes equal feast,
To churn forth funeral plumes along the shore
Of salt-plowed Carthage, then turn back for more.
Fair Nefertiti (Yes? Perhaps!) then knew the flame;
One-eyed or two, all burned to chars her fame;
Her profile, infamous, her beauty bright

A thousand tigers' eyes fireworked the night.
And Cleopatra, Caesar's cat, her ticket, too,
Was taken, torn, ignited, spread like smoking dew
On lip of Sphinx which asks and answers: What
Burns faster, finer: Bubastis? Thoth? Anubis? Set? or Tut?
Above remote Baghdad their farblown charsoots sail
Where old soothsayers spy them, spin a tale
Of mummy-dragon breaths across the stars
And Cleopatra's heart fixed fiery bright as Mars
As off the engines of destruction smote and strode
And in proud chariot fires the ancient pharaohs rode.
In fine incense and smoke they draughted, shimmered,
    blew
And all the bright Egyptian winds of time bestrew
To flag downwind through Alexandrian East
Until mid-feast some New Year later on
A Faisal in his palace, cool, Arabian-kept at dawn
Unslept and suddenly panicked and cold
For no good reason at all, sat up and wept,
Called out to the wind, afraid to die.
Then raised one trembling hand to find and pluck
The last offending soot of Nefertiti's flesh
From out his weeping eye.

Those people are not real, they're ghosts
Along the coasts of places, near or far.
They live, mere spirits at my beck and call;
I know in my Ouija heart they do not live at all.
Oh, I may beckon them—I reckon they have voices;
When my choices are to let them live, they live;
I give them sustenance by simply dialing through—
They answer from dim midnight places
But lack faces, are mere utterance, pulsed sound.
I give them territorial ground on starspun wire,
I hire them for the night and pay the fee;
They give their thoughts to me from bloodless flesh.
I summon them from Cork or Marrakesh or York or Bath,
They sound their joy or wrath to me, but what of that?
They are the dead that distance buries 'round the earth.
And yet—they live! For traveling will give them birth!
If I arrive, by God, these ghosts then rear themselves alive,
To take on garmentings of blood and flesh and skin,
Confetti-celebrate my coming there,
Arrive all Puritan, depart all sin.
For if I so desire to take my ghosts to bed,
The haunts I heard on phones now leave the dead
To put on faces, mouths, good listening ears, bright eyes.
As long as I stay on, none of them dies.
But, let me turn my back, begone, depart,

Then every loving one gives up his beating heart.
I wander off to phone from distant coasts.
My friends left there?
Go back to being . . .
. . . ghosts.

They speak beneath their breath;
They talk in tongues which wither souls,
They linger long on tombs and graveyards,
Earth and politics-by-night and moles which dig the dark;
Their park is marbled with old names,
Old times, old dooms,
They have no rooms to let to Life,
Nor any blood nor heat.
The street they shamble on is empty, long and lone,
They moan when they exhale
And with each inhalation cry;
When I say "Live," they look astonished and repeat:
Never to have been born is best,
Put down and die.

I will not hear them, cannot bear them, will not try
To even understand
How living up above
They would prefer to sleep beneath the land.
So these cold ones that fail at being warm
Would harm the world with swords of ice and doubt.
While I in Eden stand and wonder, shake my head,
And wait for God to *throw* them out!

Strange tryst was that from which stillborn
I still knew life midsummer morn,
And son of Emily/Edgar both
Did suck dry teat and swill sour broth,
And midnight know when noon was there,
And every summer breeze forswear.
Gone blind from stars and dark of moon
This boychild grew from wry cocoon;
For I was spun from spider hands
And misconceived in Usher Lands,
And all of Edgar's nightmares mine
And Em's dust-heart my valentine.
Thus mute old maid and maniac
Then birthed me forth to cataract—
That whirlpool sucked to darkest star
Where all the unborn children are.
So I was torn from maelstrom flesh
And saw in X-ray warp and mesh
A sigh of polar-region breath
That whispered skull-and-socket death.
Em could not stop for Death, so Poe
Meandered graveyards to and fro
And laid his tombstone marble bride
As Jekyll copulated Hyde
And birthed a panic-terror son.
And thus was I, mid-night, begun.

Lo, the ghost of our least favorite Uncle!
For he drank and he fell and he swore.
We could hardly wait up for his death knell,
When it came we said: "Great! What a bore!"
We could hardly hold breath for his funeral,
And we rushed him pellmell to the green,
And we buried him most uncontritely,
In the fastest performance yet seen.
And we danced a pig-jig in the summer
And we laughed when we thought of next fall
When our mostly unfavorite Uncle
Would not be around us at *all!*
And we drove in a flash and a flurry
In a hurry of motor to town
To celebrate Uncle's entombment
With dandelion wine all around.
But our smiles and our joys were foreshortened
As soon after that burial day
A ghost that resembled our Uncle
Arrived one dark midnight to stay.
My grandma found him in the coal-bin
With his scuppers full up on noon wine,
And my grandpa spied him in the attic
Where the weather of ancient was fine.
And me-myself-I saw him hanging
On a hook in the closet full-length,
And my brother swore Unk was ghost-monkey

Who swarmed the night oak-tree for strength.
At dusk when the old apples rattled
Torn loose by the wind, tossed to roof,
They ran like a caper of ghost-feet
And stomped on the dark earth like hoof.
Whatever the sound, *that* was Uncle,
Whatever the whisper or breath;
If a mouse came for cheese in the pantry
It was a small visit from Death.
Or late nights when the ice dripped from icebox
To fall in the drip-pan below
And our dog lapped the clear snowy waters,
Those sounds were my Uncle, I *know*.
And when wind turned a corner of Nowhere
And leaned on our house for a rest,
All those creakings and groanings of timber
Were the death throes of Uncle, unblessed.
So one night I got up with a candle
And crept to the foot of the stair,
And saw huddled there in each shadow
A lurk that old Death had put there.
So I revved up my shouter and screamer
To shake dust from the eaves to the bin
And I yelled: "Get! Go! Leave with your hauntings!
Go bury yourself, Uncle Sin!"
And the creeps and the shades and the shambles
Gave a shake and a mourn and a yawn

And with moaning, ochoning, lamenting
Ran off down the red crack of dawn.
And the household, aroused in their bedclothes,
Who'd heard this small boychild's uproar,
Sat up with wild smiles and applauded
Or beat their old canes on the floor.
And from that night to this: no more hauntings,
And my family lived just to boast
That a twelve-year-old boy with a loud mouth
Had slaughtered the pale family ghost.

Where my clamor was always a nuisance
And my loudness was always a sin,
I'm now the loud pal, pride, and pleasure
Of my soft-spoken kith and mute kin.

Moby Dick was two books written between
February 1850 and August 1851.
The first book did not contain Ahab.
It may not, except incidentally, have contained Moby Dick.
Somewhere along the way to writing a book about the Whale
Fishery, Melville found and bought a seven-volume set
of Shakespeare's plays. He reported on his find to his editor:

*It is an edition in glorious great type, every letter whereof is a soldier, &
the top of every 't' like a musket barrel.*
*I am mad to think how minute a cause has prevented me hitherto from
reading Shakespeare. But until now any copy that was come-at-able to
me happened to be a vile small print unendurable to my eyes which are
tender as young sperms.*
*But chancing to fall in with this glorious edition, I now exult over it,
page by page.*

Whereupon, Melville tossed his first version of The Whale overboard
and vomited forth the novel that we now know as *Moby Dick.*

At first there were but whales
And now a Whale.
At first there was but sea and tides by night
But now the fountains of Versailles somehow set sail
And sprinkled all the vasty deeps at three a.m.
With souls' pure jets.
At first there was no captain to the ship
Which, named Pequod,
Set sail for destinations, not for God.
But: God obtruded, rose and blew his breath
And Ahab rose, full born, to follow Death,
Know dark opinions,

Seek in the strangest salt dominions for one Beast
And from what was a simple-minded breakfast,
O Jesus mild and tempered sweetmeats,
Now a Feast!

How came it so?
That from such crumbs tossed forth at morning
Such great nightmare terrors grow,
What was a cat-toy lost upon old summer lawns
Has through one season grown to monster size
To panic-color all gray Melville's dawns?

Why, Willie happened by!
That is the end, the explanation, and the all.
As blind almost as Homer, Herman never read
The good or bad or in-between Othello
The dead put down by Richard Third,
Iago's boast,
Never, gone out at midnight in his mind,
Had Ahab with a small a
Stumbled and fallen blind against
Mad Hamlet's father's murdered ghost.
But now, in seven volumes of large size
And large, O gods, the font of type,
The words, the trumpetings of metaphor and doom:
All that was microscopic filled his room,
All that had filled his room now filled his mind

From south to west then east and now the panicked North.
Shakespeare beneath his window gave his shout:
"O Lazarus! Herman Melville! truly come ye forth!
And what's that *with* you?
Dreadful gossamer?
Funeral wake? or Arctic veil?"
"What, this? Why, Jesus lily-of-the-valley breath,
It seems to be . . .
A Whale!"

And what a whale! A trueborn Beast of God.
Shakespeare stood back away
As Herman trod a path and made a launching-spot, a maze
Wherein to lose then find titanic Moby
And then *send him down the ways!*
And then an ancient King came forth to stand with Will
And call along the tide of Time down hill along the wind
And tear his beard and rend his sanity,
Disclaim his daughters, curse all midnight Fates.
So Lear and his progenitor gave cry
And from an Arctic miracle of waters
A white shape formed to panic and to most delicious fright,
A whale like all Antarctica, dread avalanche of dawn at night
Ribbed, skinned, then stuffed with lights and soul filched out
    of Lear
Sailed, submarine, through Richard Third's wild dreams,
Touched Verne, and maddened Freud and kept our schemes,

Those schemes American which were, while awed,
To question all the malt that Milton drank while sipping God.
God, Nature, Space, all Time, now stand aside, we said.
The Whale, in answer, gasping, fluming Universal breath
Rushed at us like a marbled tomb, his spout one bloody fount
    of Death.
And rammed and sank our hubris, fluked our pride.
The waters shut and closed on all who died that day on the
    Pequod.
So the American men, each one proclaimed self-king
Took their blasphemies beneath the monstrous watering
While Ahab wrapped in hemp upon his cumbrous bride
Still beckoning to us to follow, worry, harrow
Those tracks that watery vanish on the instant trod,
With one last outraged cry, a fisting wave,
Sank from our view with God.

So Melville in his inner deeps did dive
To find the shroud, the ghost, the thing alive
In all the flesh that, aged, shadowed, dead
Most wanted issue, to be found, known, read,
And on the lawns of Avon took his stance
To join the Bard in festive, antic dance.
And to the morning window of old Will
As morn came up and dusk went down the sill
Cried out, O Lazarus William Shakespeare,
Come *you* forth in whale!

And Will all fleshed in marble white
Could not prevail against such summonings and taunts,
And slid him forth in size for jaunts to break a continent,
Sink Armadas in the tides.
So Shakespeare glides forever in dread comet tails
That shine the Deeps,
He prowls that mutual subterrane
Where Melville/God's truth starts and wakes from murdered
    sleeps.

Thus from his antique caul, his bloody veil
Old Willie William, long gone dust in jail,
Was clamored forth to freedom in a Whale
That swam all thunders, rumors, plunders in the morn,
Insurance that good Shakespeare, now reborn,
Would live two lives, the one he'd had before
But now another chance to make less More.
From blubbers, metals, renderings he rose
To dress plain-suited Melville in fresh clothes,
Such clothes as foreskin whale-prick metaphors can make
    and sell,
Illumine Heaven and relight the coals of Hell.
So Shakespeare, boned and fleshed and marrowed deep
Did waken Melville from whale-industries of sleep
To run on water, burn St. Elmo's fires,
And shape cathedral spires from Moby's titan rib-cage
    tossed to shore

And again and again from less make feasts of More.
What was mere oil of spermaceti now became
Anointments for a Papal brow in Sweet Christ's name
Pronounced from drippings of fused universal mask and
      face,
What first was simple journeying became a Chase.
So off and round the world ran two men, wild,
Skinned in one Lazarus flesh, one loud, one mild,
Each summoning the other,
And neither knowing which was elder, therefore evil-wiser
      brother
Until—Flukes out! black blood!
From mutual toil
They brought a miracle of fish to boil;
Like God who spoke and uttered Light,
These twins in unison said Night
And there was Night;
That night in which great panics birthed and hid,
That dawnless hour from which old Moby slid
And knocked the world half off its axis into awe
And all because Dear Willie stuck his metaphor down
      Herman's craw!

One hundred years from now, in 2075, all England lies empty.
Her people have left, gone off to find the sun in Rome, Nairobi, Rio de
Janeiro, and San Diego, California.
Left behind in the empty land is one man, a poet.
He finds that, in Westminster, even the Stone of Scone, upon which most
of England's rulers have been crowned, is gone.
The Royal Family has taken it with them to warmer lands in southern
climes.
The poet speaks:

The Stone, the Stone of Scone, you say?
They've shipped it south to Summer's Bay?
Aye, that, that holy rock, that Stone,
They've mailed it off, it's gone, it's flown;
And Westminster, this day at dawn
Is empty as old Blenheim's lawn.
And gone our Kings from winter's sill,
And gone our Queens from autumn's chill,
And with them vanish common folk
Who once took winter for a joke,
But now are summoned by those Souths
That melt old jokes like ice in mouths;
And, suntanned, jolly, called by May
They up and soared their souls away;
Wild credit cards and borrowed crown
Have lured and laughed them out of town.
They've gone to tan and tint their flanks

Midst sunburned Aussies, surfing Yanks,
And England, left behind alone,
Has naught to sit on save the Stone,
But now *that's* gone, that's borrowed, too?
Yes! And the villages are few
Where even sparrows come in choirs
And few the Stonehenge midnight fires
Of ghosts that gather in to tell
A mystery of Time and Will
When monarchs chilled their bums here still
And did not rule bereft, alone,
But from the lofty perch of Scone
Looked out upon a Kipling Land
Where regal Queens shone up the Strand.

So then in Westminster I'll preen
Where ruddy Rudyard bowed a queen
And I will walk and snuff the dust
That once was old Macaulay's lust
And tread on Pope, and Johnson know,
Their relics stashed in vaults below.
Then when lights dim and dawn's at hand
I'll search about Victoria's land
And find me rock and beg a loan
And chisel me new Scottish Scone
And haul it down the empty aisle
And seat me there, Royal Son, awhile.

And from a snake in winter's path
Make up a crown half joy, half wrath
And place it on my funeral brow
To cover up my winter snow,
And wreathe myself with ancient spring
And name myself the Final King,
The Ninth and Final Henry here
In vanished pomps, in melted year,
And sleep me out on tomb-top there
A statue on my own hard bier
To rest before I make the rounds
As bellman to all London's towns
Who pulls the ropes in farflung towers
To sound the Sad Year's final hours.
While to the dead long lost turned clay
This pledge and promise then I'll say:

Elizabeths, rare One, mild Two,
I send this message back to you,
I'll keep the Island fast for thee,
Defenseless she will never be.
I'll tread upon the chalky shore
To toss back Hitler's men, and more:
Will sword away the Viking host
And guard each mineless deep, each coast
Where only seagulls knife the dawn.
And I will up and mow the lawn

At Buckingham, and pull the weed
And not let England go to seed.
All this I promise, ladies, dead,
I to your memory am wed,
I husband history-gone-to-sleep
And will your green land roam and keep,
A single lonely lover I
My own Armada, fresh and spry
Will all of Thames' sweep free of death
And in the springtime's vernal breath
Leap up from chalk cliff with my wings
And Spitfire-like make harvestings
Of all Mad Adolf's Fokker-men
Who would blood England down again.
So Army-Navy-R.A.F.
I'll poise upon the Dover cliff
And now be sailor, now be men
Such as will ne'er be seen again,
As Churchill spoke them in the blue:
"So many saved by, God, so few."

And when I've won the wars of Rose
I'll in the Avon round compose
And rear up Richard, Hamlet doubt,
Then with them all Time put to rout;
And saved the land, and saved our seed,
Do with my dreams a new race breed.

O little England, lost at sea,
I give my single self to thee,
When all and each is gone or dead,
I stand as shining figurehead
And shall be King if it need be
And populate your towns for thee
With children's dreams, my memories,
My Horse Guard phantoms trotting through
May not disturb one mote of dew,
Yet jog they will, and off they go
And Hadrian and Caesar know,
And cry the Roman Roads at night
And beckon me to join their fight.
O One and Two Elizabeths,
Yours not the only Royal deaths,
For by you now the whole land lies
And storms weep out my outraged eyes.

Enough! I will not burn my mind
I turn about, away, half blind,
And on my fresh-cut Stone of Scone
Write: Britain's Population? One.
But that one millions represents,
The sinners, and the innocents,
And Shakespeare, Pope, and Dryden, too,
And Dickens, Wycherley drum through
Beneath my window every dawn

To summon me to tread the lawn
For one more journey round the Isle
And all them with me mile on mile;
So round about from south to north
And spyglassing the Firth of Forth,
And compassing dire Scotland, Wales
To from grim ancient stocks and gaols
Fetch pensioners and poor to coasts
That must tide back the Spanish hosts.
And in Trafalgar New Year's Eve
Will gently joy, and gently grieve . . .

But, here! I'm running on again.
I must be off! It looks like rain.

O son, farewell, get off the Isle,
And let me walk and think awhile;
Go south to all those Afrique lands,
To golden shores and blazing sands
And say that Henry sends his best
And all our strewn seed now is blessed
By mad King pacing here alone
To guard his proxy Stone of Scone.
Then sing some Auld Lang Syne for me
In equatorial summer sea,
And I will sing back Auld Lang Syne
And Blood and Sweat and Tears, now mine,

And be the bulldog to lost Queen
And gardener to all the green
At Blenheim where, tomorrow morn
Who knows? old Churchill is reborn
To start the wheels of Time again
And populate the Land with rain
Of people showering from the sky
To certain-sure Queen Mab won't die.

O populations, fled away
To gift yourself with lasting day
And kept by summers that shan't end,
I here your last live blood defend.
You go with sun. I stay with snow.
You bed with heat. I winters know.
Stay there, warm flesh, where you have flown.
Forgiving, I, mad, crowned, alone,
Keep warm thy proxy Stone of Scone.

The syncopated hunchbacked man
He moves in rhythms all his own,
The bone along his back does this to him,
He moves then to a private inner whim
A hymn to cartilage, a spine that broke
By sheer genetics in the womb, God's hidden joke;
So balled into the world he came and soon or late
His shellcrab shoulders taught his bones to syncopate
And pat and shuffle on the street as if to fling
Him in a rigadoon of spring; he comes
And pressured is his mouth in whines and hums;
A *Gloria* perhaps to chromosome
That built him from cracked bricks, a cramping home
In which his soul like doll is stuffed in house
The house a caving roof, his soul crazed mouse
That hides in blood then rushes and collides
With yet more crumpled bone, a rodent mad
With gyrating, while up above? A face that's glad.
A mask? But no. The hunchback loves the fall,
The summer, winter, spring, he takes it all,
It's one romance;
And where his spine taught him to shuffle-tap and syncopate
Now realer dance does seize his feet
And in an ecstasy of life, goes down the street.
So Being, if even it's hunched, finds recompense
And dearly loves June miracles immense;
For Christ Himself, who knows? once shared this lack:
Born, lived, laughed, wept, and died, with crumpled back.

What size is Space? A thimble!
No! outside of a Sun!
The nimble tricks of lightning,
Dichotomies lost, won;
Black holes in which, sequestered,
Great nightmares stride the beams,
Sun-spots in which gods, festered,
Give up their fractured dreams.
What is this dream of Cosmos,
What's birthed from Panic's plan?
A mad brave wingless bird-thing,
This beast half-grown to Man.
Born from a senseless yearning
Of molecules for form,
Birthed from a mindless burning
Of solar fire-storm—
The Universe, in needing,
Made flesh of empty space,
And with a mighty seeding
Made pygmy human race . . .
Which now on fires striding
Walks up the stars to live
And cry to God in hiding:
We birth ourselves! Forgive!
Then from the Cosmos breathing,
An answering word from Him:
"No, dwarf-child, self-bequeathing,

I birthed *you* as a whim.
I laughed you from the darkness,
I dropped you as a joke,
But, strange, small, fragile creature,
You fell but never broke!
And now I see you laughing
As if the joke were yours;
Perhaps we made each other
In some wild common cause.
So let us share a hubris,
Take common flesh as bread,
And drink each other's laughter,
Fall from each other's bed.
But, careful, darling monster,
Your laugh might crack your soul,
What's yours is mine, remember,
We, separate, are Whole."
God laughs, and Man gives answer,
Man laughs and God responds;
Then off they glide on rafters
Of stars like skating-ponds.
And which is God, which Human,
Let God now truly say:
"We fly much like each other,
We walk a common clay.
I dreamed Man into being,
He dreams Me now to stay—

Twin mirror selves of seeing,
We live Forever's Day.
If Man should die I'd blindly
Rebirth that Beast again;
I cannot live without him.
Man dead? Then God is slain!
My Universe needs seeing,
That's Man's eternal task,
What is the use of being,
If God is but a mask?"
So, Man and God, conjoining,
Are One, uncelibate,
And spawn the Cosmic rivers,
In billions celebrate
No Ending or Beginning,
No crease, stitch, fold or seam;
Where God leaves off, Man's starting
To recompense the Dream.
Behold! the Mystery stirring . . .
Here come the human moles!
To rise behind God's masking
And peek out from the holes.

Othello's occupations?
Here they lie—in countries where the spacemen
Flow in fire and much desire the Moon
And reach for Mars,
And teach the fiery atoms how to sing
And bring intemperate blood to God-lost lands
To warm His snow-frost lunar sands
And never ask: To Be Or Not To Be,
For here all Is and Is Again, at our behest.
Mind's quest makes footfall here
For transfer across Space to lift Mankind.
Long blind, we catwalk breadths and heights,
Fix sights in rare Assembly shop as vast as Shakespeare's mind
And add that Melville once drowsed here
To dream the Beast awake;
Pumped lox for blood and with one quake
Of God's triumphant voice made rocket blast
Thus rousing lunar whale to swim in star-tides vast.

How then describe how high, how wide, how wild
This fire-fiord place?
Tape-measure Shakespeare's brow
Night-travel nineteen light-years deep and down
Pale Hamlet's face.
Sweet William long years dead? No, no.
Step through this labyrinth portal
Stand slaking Eden's breath, immortal;
Where Saturn, born to new Hells, learns his lust,

Where Titan resurrected now is thrust
Across the comet-midwife light-year poet's skull. Not dead.
The brow that knows itself and knows it knows,
The thought that birthed itself to Space
Where now Man goes.
Not dead, no, no, not dead.
Name it Canaveral/Kennedy/Stratford? More! Instead
Say: Shakespeare's Life-Force, God's dream,
Church-cathedral head.

Then will this solid flesh downfall, resolve itself in dew?
No! Yeast that solid flesh, resolve it to a fire
Conspire to know and build and try
For if God's dead, then Man can surely die.
But All being One (it is! it *is!*)
God/Man/Ghost takes as bride
Entire Comet Universe to yoke with pride
And seed-bed Moon and mouth-breathe Mars
With child/boy/men in bright new Ra Egyptian fire-chariot
    cars.

Put out the light and then put out the light?
Stay. Kindle night and then rekindle night.
Othello unemployed, now reemployed
To summon racial memory from Jung and Freud
And in genetics' marrow seek God's Will
To find lost man and send him up the hill
Of stars to change the dreadful dates of 1984

And sum them up with shouts to make a score
Man could not dream or hope or care to do;
Make Orwell *laugh* in year 2002!

Grand Things to Come? Yes! Things to Come!
Cabal stands here! that towering son of Wells who saw a sea
Of wheeling orbs and sparks and cried:
Which shall it be?
Sink back to dust and tomb, to worms and grave,
Or onward to dead Mars and Mankind save?
And star-blown winds now echo endlessly:
Which shall it be, O wandering man, which shall,
Which shall it be?

Will Shakespeare dead? No, no!
This *is* his place I tread, his time and flight and dream
His corridors of night, his islands lost in time
His thunders, rumors, questionings of self:
To be or not to be on Saturn's shelf.
Not lost? No, no, not lost in dust or rain
Or falling down of years.
From Yorick's skull, God's manifesto peers;
From graveyard dirt he shapes a striding man
To jig the stars and go where none else can.

What pulls him there in arrow flights of ships?
A birth of suns that burn from Shakespeare's flaming lips.
Not dumb dull TV news inspires lost man

But Will who, turned in sleeps, earthquakes our plan
And answers Job whose agonies and sulks ask why
This fragile flesh is thrust forth cold to die?
Not so! says Pleiades for tongue,
Not so! Not so!
From Stratford's fortress mind we build and go
And strutwork catwalk stars across abyss
And to small wondering seed-bed souls do promise this:
To Be is best, and Not to Be far worse.
And Will says what?
Stand here, grow tall, rehearse.
Be God-grown-Man.
Act out the Universe!

The graveyard man is almost old. But, no,
Same age as I. He only seems an older twin
Because his sin, to me at least, is digging. Or—much worse:
The hearse takes not his mind.
He never thinks on death, he's far too fond of work for that.
He wears his ancient hat askew,
His look makes windowpane of you. You are not there.
Today, tomorrow, yesterday, all one.
Because his work is never done, I sense some small
    resentment;
I've come to find the brother lost before my birth,
The grandfather I grieved when I was six;
In all this mix of rococo-baroque, where do they hide?
"Well, now, let's see. What month? What day?"
The man trots out of sun. I follow him to find
No great charts showing sunken lands of death.
Some old notebooks make do, much gone to hair and
    raveling.
His earth-dark finger traveling the pages
Touches Palmer Penmanship of other years
Which names the lost whose Finder Dark has stashed them
    here.
I cannot name the year or hour for him. I stopped here on
    a whim.
Cross-country midnight on a train I thought I heard
My grandpa call again,
Thought I heard my brother laugh from flowered green.

All this now seems obscene by day.
The digger's finger jabs and points to touch and stay
At Baby Addison, Baby Simms, Baby Jones, too much, too
    much!
That was a time of buried young,
Death sprinkled them like frozen seed,
He gave no heed to medicines, for there were none.
The brightest, smallest sparks of sun extinguished he;
And nameless let them fall.   The 1918/1919 stones read,
    all about:
CHILD.   SIX MONTHS.   THREE MONTHS.   ONE YEAR.
No first names given.   These lost were barely born.
Leave them to Heaven.
The old man stops to touch my grandpa's name,
And then a boy named Sam.
I wonder if I'm sad. I think I am.
We go to find the plot and see but space,
No stone to grace the small or large bones here,
They did consign my relatives to wind and rain
And dandelion.
Well, then, did they love less, who put no chiseled rock
To mark these lost? What would have been the cost?
No matter if they came and shameless dropped their tears
To rinse these souls in buried years.
And now here, I, kneeled down in springtime-day-turned-fall
And suddenly not large or old but young and small,
Put forth my hand to let them know

That I am here who loved them so.
I break a flower and use its stem
To write the names and dates of those who slept
And now at last have names and dates.
The hour grows late. I run. Outside the gates
I turn and, glorious God!
On distant green and lonely sod
I still can see the mark I've made
To light their dark-in-spring-noon shade;
Their names in dust, their dates in grass
Erased by shadow clouds that pass,
Their headstone one bright gift of mine:
A blazing summer dandelion.

Oh, the bad that I've demolished, they are doing far too well,

And the bores that I have vanquished now have learned
new ways to spell;

For the alphabet of tombstones, once it's learned, can set
you free,

So these nonbook, awful writers now turn up to blab at tea.

Lo, the Fascists and the Commies, Richard's Plumbers in a
Clan,

All the jet-set hostage-killers that forever frighten man,

Clang their death-bells, shriek for banknotes, every night
upon my lawn

After all my time invested to make super-sure they'd gone.

For from Hell where I had sent them now the driveling
fiends return

In the vapored rains of fire where dire Savonarolas burn,

Here come Sirhan Sirhan cabals, Senate Girl-Friends whose
élan

Marches Dante down the sludgeways where new novels hit
the fan.

Here Mad Donkey, sad Behemoth (G.O.P. upon his flank)

Ballot-stuffers, candle-muffers of the meanest row and rank,

Here runs night-train bearing Lenin, there kind Stalin and
his mob,

Here, reprinted, *Adolf's Bunker*; Mayor Daley (Lyndon's
slob),

Hail, John Dean, John Mitchell, Agnew—live best-sellers in
the stalls,

While more lecturing assassins fill our cities' concert halls.
So, in death there seems much living, and in evil mostly good.
Otherwise why do these demons Watergate my neighbor-
hood?

God, more books about young Edward sunk near Chappa-
quiddick Bridge,
One more second-gunman theory on the Dallas Book-
Tower ridge!
Linda Lovelace, be our teacher, *Hustler* Flynt now be our
scribe,
Martin Bormann, Hess and Goebbels, all's forgiven! Lead
our tribe!
Orwell taught us black was whiter if you stood upon your
head,
Now we know that white is blacker and what's most alive
is dead.
All kidnappers and skyjackers, get you home and write a
book!
But be sure the title reads as: *Heck, You Know That I'm No
Crook.*
Franco's dead—Ah, God, the wonder! Look! Indira Gandhi's
gone!
But ten books about these monsters will be done and out
by dawn!

So I'll retire me to Bedlam, for my goodness is my shame,
Or I'll hire some evil Berlitz, teach myself a smarter game,

Run with dogs and hogs and butchers, make Caligula my
name;
Vote for Nixon, Mao, Castro, Idi Amin, James Earl Ray.
Buy a bedsheet, cut some eyeholes, join the Book Club KKK.
Kill Olympic sports for breakfast, burn an airport, see the
sights!
Then send cables, ask for bidders, sell the film and TV rights.
Patty Hearst is ripe for sequels, flood the market, what the
hell.
Since the bad that I once vanquished, still around, are
doing well.

A NOTE ABOUT THE TYPE

This book was set in the film version of Optima, a typeface designed by Hermann Zapf from 1952 to 1955 and issued in 1958. In designing Optima, Zapf created a truly new type form—a cross between the classic roman and a sans-serif face. So delicate are the stresses and balances in Optima that it rivals sans-serif faces in clarity and freshness and old-style faces in variety and interest.

Composed by Monotype Composition Company, Inc., Baltimore, Maryland; printed and bound by American Book–Stratford Press, Saddle Brook, New Jersey. Typography based on a design by Clint Anglin. Binding design by Camilla Filancia.